ECHOES

of
world
war
II

ECHOES

of world war II

Trish Marx

Lerner Publications Company • Minneapolis, Minnesota

To Patrick, Molly, and Annie, my inspiration,
Owen, my motivation,
and those in this book, my education

This edition published in 1994 by:
Lerner Publications Company
241 First Avenue North
Minneapolis, MN 55401

First published in 1989 by Macdonald Children's Books
Simon & Schuster International Group
Wolsey House, Wolsey Road
Hemel Hempstead, England, HP2 4SS

Library of Congress Cataloging-in-Publication Data

Marx, Trish.
    Echoes of World War Two / by Trish Marx.
        p.   cm.
    "First published in 1989 by Macdonald Children's
Books…Hemel Hempstead"–T.p. verso.
    Includes index.
    Summary: Presents the stories of six people from different
parts of the world whose childhoods were shaped by their
experiences during World War II.
    ISBN 0-8225-4898-4
    1. World War, 1939-1945–Children–Juvenile literature.
2. World War, 1939-1945–Personal narratives–Juvenile
literature. [1. World War, 1939-1945–Personal narratives.]
I. Title. II. Title: Echoes of World War II. III. Title: Echoes
of World War II.
D810.C4M37   1994
940.53'161–dc20   92-47369
CIP
AC

Manufactured in the United States of America
    2   3   4   5   6 – P/JR – 99 98 97 96 95

Contents

tions and were forced to do heavy labor. Eventually, Hitler used many of the camps to systematically execute millions of people.

The Levys, like many other Jewish families, were forced to move from place to place in an attempt to escape Hitler's persecution. Anti-Jewish feeling reached frightening proportions on November 9, 1938, when a national demonstration against Jews became extremely violent, resulting in what is now known as Kristallnacht, the night of broken glass.

Hitler declared his party, the National Socialist (Nazi) Party, the only legal political party in Germany and planned to conquer all of Europe. Germany invaded Poland on September 1, 1939, and Britain and France declared war on Germany two days later. In May of 1940, Germany invaded Holland from the south. Hitler's Blitzkrieg, or lightning war, used land and air forces to overrun countries by speed and surprise. By the middle of 1940, Germany controlled Poland, Austria, France, Holland, Belgium, Denmark, Norway, and Czechoslovakia. All Jewish people in these nations were in danger of capture and deportation to concentration camps in the east.

Germany fell to the Allied forces (the United States, Britain, France, and the Soviet Union) in 1945. Six million Jews had been killed in the death camps or trying to flee the Nazis. But some fortunate Jews, like Hans Levy, survived the Nazi persecution because of brave gentiles like Mrs. Gertrude Wijsmuller, who risked her own life hiding Jews from the Nazis. Mrs. Wijsmuller is remembered today at Yad Vashem, the museum and library in Israel dedicated to victims of the Holocaust.

Amongst the rubble I saw the heavy brass Chanukia gleaming in the semi-darkness of the room. I picked it up and put it on the table, covered by a torn tablecloth. . . . It was that night my parents resolved to send us away.

Solomon Levy lit the Hanukkah candles and looked across the table. Oskar, Hans, and Elsbeth looked solemn, but their eyes were shining with excitement. They loved the Hanukkah dinner, served on the family's best starched tablecloth, with wine in crystal glasses. Six-year-old Hans smiled at his

1939: A Jewish refugee family walks through the streets of Memel, Germany, as Nazi officers in the background jeer.

mother as she ladled his soup into a delicate china bowl. Right then, he felt that everything he needed or could want was in that room.

But only a few months later, Hans returned from school to find a strange car parked outside the house. The car belonged to the Gestapo—Hitler's secret police.

The windows of the family grocery store had been smashed. The shop had been ransacked. "Don't buy from Jews" had been scrawled on the door.

The Levy family abandoned what was left of their shop and their home and fled to another town. This was just the first of many moves for the Levys. Hans's father took a new job.

Map indicates early World War II borders (1939-1942)

My father traveled all over Germany selling wines. He went mainly to farmers, but of course, never told anybody his real name, as Levy is a very Jewish name. If they had found out he was Jewish he would never have made a living.

As Hitler's policy of anti-Semitism grew, life for the Levys became more and more difficult. By 1935, Hans could no longer go to the movies or swim in the public swimming pool. He was often called a "dirty Jew."

One day I went to the butcher to pick up some meat for my mother. A customer dropped something from her purse and, as a gentleman, I stopped to pick it up. I heard "Don't you touch that." This is not just my story. Every Jewish person tells these stories.

The Levys' landlord worked for the railroad—which threatened to fire him if he continued renting to a Jewish family. The Levys were once again forced to move out of their home.

Hans was just falling asleep one night when he heard the crashes of windows being shattered and doors being forced open. He heard his neighbor shouting and a man cry out in agony. He wiggled deeper under his covers and pulled the pillow over his head, afraid to move, afraid almost to breathe. Then he heard his own windows break and his parents' voices from downstairs, sounding harsh and frightened. Heavy steps fell on the stairway and his bedroom door flew open.

The light went on and there stood this huge figure, in the all-too-familiar black SS [Nazi] uniform. I tried to shout for my parents, but in terror my vocal cords were completely blocked. I just slid under my blankets as this giant walked toward me. Probably realizing my age, he told me how lucky I was and then left the room. I learned later the man screaming was my uncle. He had been beaten with a horsewhip.

This was *Kristallnacht*: November 9, 1938, the "night of broken glass" in Hitler's Germany. It was the Nazi party's first violent nationwide attack on the Jewish people.

The soldier left Hans terrified, but he knew the immediate danger was gone. He wondered about his precious gramophone (record player), the only possession he was allowed to bring each time his family moved in their futile attempts to find peace.

> The next morning we went downstairs to assess the damage. Every window on the ground floor had been broken, the living room was in absolute shambles. The cupboards had been overturned and lying in shatters were family heirlooms of glass and china from a century ago. Chairs and settees were ripped open. But they had not touched my precious gramophone, in a cabinet of ebony. It still stood next to the overturned cupboard.

Hans's parents, Solomon and Helene Levy, thought of themselves primarily as Germans whose faith was Jewish. Like other German Jews, they fought alongside their fellow Germans in World War I (1914–1918), and suffered with them in the depression that followed that war. Now all they wanted was to raise their three children to be loyal Germans who would someday use their skills

Adolf Hitler at a Nazi rally in Nuremberg, Germany

In April 1933, a boycott against Jewish merchants was announced. The sign reads "Germans, defend yourselves, do not buy from Jews."

A bedroom ransacked
during Kristallnacht

and knowledge to Germany's benefit. But the Nazis saw the Levys as Jews—not Germans. Kristallnacht was a warning to Hans's parents, a warning that Solomon heeded.

> A neighbor drove up and asked my father and uncle to go with him, to God knows where, as he thought their lives might be in danger. We [Hans, Oskar, Elsbeth, and their mother] moved in with the neighbor's wife and children. The first night we spent in a small lumber room, sitting on boxes. During the night we could hear the SS searching the house. At one time they tried the door of the room but did not persist. The days that followed began a series of interrogations, sometimes two, three, or four a day, asking where the men were.

Hans's father came back a few weeks later, tired and dirty. He had gone to a neighboring village to stay with a great-aunt, but he gave himself up when the SS swept through the village. On the way, he had seen synagogues and homes burning and had realized how widespread Kristallnacht had been. After this ordeal, Solomon and Helene resolved to find a way to send their children out of Germany.

The demolished sanctuary of a German synagogue

The opportunity came only a few weeks later, in January 1939. The Jewish Refugee Committee, a volunteer organization formed by the German Jewish community during the war, organized a train of children to be transported to Amsterdam, Holland. Hans, Oskar, and Elsbeth Levy, each with a suitcase of new clothes, were on that train. The family believed they would be reunited and talked of plans for the future. But the Nazis continued to make life difficult for Jews. Solomon and Helene were repeatedly denied the right to leave Germany.

Hans, Oskar, and Elsbeth spent the next 16 months in Amsterdam. "The Dutch people were fantastic," Hans recalled. "They took us in and housed us in one of their holiday homes for orphans." Elsbeth was sent to a girls' hostel outside of Amsterdam.

Hans's and Oskar's only communication with their parents came from 25-word messages sent through neutral Switzerland by the International Red

Cross. These Red Cross letters often took weeks to arrive. Yet they were the only way thousands of war victims could hope to keep in touch with their families, which were often scattered all over Europe.

When Germany invaded Holland in 1940, Hans, Oskar, and Elsbeth were once again in danger of being sent to concentration camps. But Hans and Oskar made a last-minute escape:

> There was a Jewish Refugee Committee in Holland, headed by a woman called Gertrude Wijsmuller, and she was a fantastic person. She played cuckoo with [outwitted] the Germans, and she got many people out of going to the concentration camps. She organized a coach and a driver and, with 60 other children, drove us to a seaport called Ijmuiden. She got us into a cargo boat. . . . It took us five days to get to England . . . the first night we were shot at by the Germans, they tried to catch us. The captain of the ship . . . decided on Liverpool . . . nobody knew we were coming, we just escaped. When we left Ijmuiden [on the cargo ship *Bodegrafen*], we saw fire burning in the city. The Germans obviously bombed some of it, and that very night Holland capitulated [surrendered]. We got out on the very, very last boat.

Jewish refugees from Germany arrive in Harwich, England.

Right, A six-year-old war orphan at Buchenwald, a German concentration camp. *Below,* Jewish refugee children arrive in the United States from Germany in 1939.

On the night Hans and Oskar escaped on the boat, Elsbeth found her way into the burning city in search of her brothers.

Luckily, we had some relatives in Amsterdam. [Not finding us,] she lived there. But eventually, they took all Jews living in Holland into concentration camps.

Elsbeth was sent to the concentration camp Theresienstadt in Sudetenland, a part of Czechoslovakia given to Germany during the war. By chance she found her mother and father among the crowds of prisoners. Solomon and Helene Levy had been arrested and sent to the camp a few years after their children fled to Holland.

My sister told a story about my parents. When she met them in Theresienstadt, the first concentration camp they were sent to, my mother was terribly ashamed of my father because he was in jail there. He had a job peeling potatoes in the kitchen and he stole a couple of potatoes. He was

Jewish families were forced to leave their homes in Nazi Germany.

Survivors of the German concentration camp Lager Nordhausen

found out and he was in jail for two or three weeks, and she was so ashamed of that.

Elsbeth was later sent to Auschwitz, a camp in Poland. She was one of the few people still alive there when the Allied forces liberated Auschwitz at the end of the war. In 1945, after writing to the orphanage in Amsterdam where Hans and Oskar had first been, Elsbeth learned her brothers were alive and had been in England for three years. She wrote to them there.

> I thought she was dead and of course there was great joy. She was in Amsterdam and we kept in touch all the time . . . of course, she told the story about our parents.

Solomon and Helene had spent three years trying to escape from Germany, to reunite their family, and to hide from the persecution. Finally, in September 1942, after spending time in Theresienstadt, they were rounded up, put on a train to Auschwitz, and almost immediately sent to the gas chamber. Elsbeth arrived in the camp later and was able to piece together their story from surviving inmates.

Hans arrived in England at the age of 12. The Jewish Refugee Committee in Manchester had purchased two houses for the children who had escaped on Mrs. Wijsmuller's boat. Hans and Oskar settled so comfortably in their new surroundings that Hans turned down a chance to be adopted by an English family, preferring to remain with Oskar.

Hans, Oskar, and Elsbeth were able to stay in touch after the war. Elsbeth helped to reunite other Jewish people—who found themselves alone and in different parts of the world after the war—with their families.

Hans is married and still lives in England. Since Elsbeth's death in 1984, Hans has carried on her work of reuniting Holocaust families. Every September he lights a candle in the synagogue in memory of Helene and Solomon Levy, who were brave enough to send their children away.

GUERLET
ANDREE PAU

ANDRÉE-PAULE MASON

Andrée-Paule Mason was born in Normandy, a region of northwestern France. Because her father was a diplomat, Andrée-Paule's family lived in many different countries while she was growing up. During the war, Andrée-Paule lived in Hungary and Sweden. She was in Paris the day that city was liberated from the Germans.

By the time Hitler took power in Germany, many people in France were tired of war. World War I had destroyed many areas of Normandy, and when World War II broke out, the repair of towns and villages had only just been completed. France fell to Germany in June 1940. After an armistice (treaty) with Germany was signed, France was divided into two zones, with Germany occupying northern France, including Paris. The southern part was unoccupied but was ruled by the Vichy government, which was established and controlled by the Germans. The Vichy government was headed by Marshal Henri Pétain and was based in the town of Vichy.

Andrée-Paule was 16 when the war started. Her age permitted her to make some decisions independently of her family. One of these was to join the French Resistance, an underground group that fought against the German occupation of France. Resistance workers who were caught could be jailed, tortured, shot, or sent to concentration camps, and their families were often given the same treatment. A Resistance fighter usually knew only one or two names of contact people, and these names were often false. This way, the captured Resistance worker would not be able to give away any important information to the enemy, even under torture.

The Resistance was headed by General Charles de Gaulle, leader of the Free French (those who fought against the occupying Vichy government). De Gaulle had escaped the Nazi invasion of France and was stationed in England. By working in small groups of people, with each group known only to the contact person, France was able to wage an effective underground war against Germany.

Because of the Resistance, thousands of Allied soldiers whose planes had crashed in the French countryside were taken to a safe shelter—a barn, shed, or back room—and then secretly sent out of the country before German troops could find them. Hundreds of bridges, railroad lines, and factories were bombed by the Resistance. Countless messages, carried by messengers like Andrée-Paule, were vital to these missions.

The Allies landed in Normandy in June 1944. Other Allied troops landed in southern France and headed north to Paris. Led by General de Gaulle and the Free French, the Allies entered and liberated the city from German occupation.

I was too young to feel I could completely break from my family, and I felt a responsibility that if I did too much my family would be in trouble. I did small things which were useful in their way, and I had a lot to be arrested for.

Andrée-Paule loved to listen to her father talk. As a diplomat with the French government, he often had access to new information. Andrée-Paule was always there to listen to her father's ideas on politics and world affairs. As a teenager, she learned from him to form strong opinions and, when World War II broke out, to make choices based on her own convictions.

France was very divided, and in many families some people fought de Gaulle and the Resistance, and some people, like my father, were for de Gaulle. To know the history of France at that time, you have to understand how complex it was in the families—families would be very divided because they had different beliefs and different emotions about whether or not France should have surrendered. From the very beginning, my father never changed his ideas, and I felt the same as he did. I was very eager when we went back to live in France to try to do something to help the Allies.

Adolf Hitler and Nazi sculptor Arno Breker pose for a movie camera in Paris, June 1940.

Map indicates early World War II borders (1939-1942)

When the armistice with the Germans was signed in 1940, many French people were relieved that they would not have to continue fighting. But Andrée-Paule's father was not happy.

> We were [posted] in Hungary at the time of the armistice. The next thing we knew Hungary was allied with the Germans. . . . We were . . . being spied upon by the authorities and followed everywhere . . . my father was always doing what he could for the Allies. . . . We knew some Poles and Czechs and they were trying to escape from Hungary. We hid them in the embassy, and I remember we tried to help them escape from there, which was very difficult because the Hungarian police were watching the building. We had to put them [the Poles and Czechs] in the boot [trunk] of the car and then free them when nobody was looking. Hungary suffered very much, but we left after the armistice [between France and Germany].

With great sadness for what was happening in France, Andrée-Paule and her family traveled to neutral Sweden. There, her father resumed his duties as a diplomat, but this time for the new Vichy government.

> Sweden was like another life, from a comfort point of view. My father thought it was interesting because everybody was spying on everybody else. He heard a lot of information about what was going on all over the world, which he could pass on . . . he sent all sorts of information to the French government . . . they were angry because at times he would tell the government they shouldn't have accepted the armistice.

Andrée-Paule's father soon realized the difficulties of working for a government he personally disagreed with. After only a few months in Sweden, he resigned from his post, and the family moved to unoccupied France. In 1942 the Germans occupied all of France, and Andrée-Paule's family moved to Paris.

In Paris, Andrée-Paule finished school and went to the university. Always aware of the tensions in France, she felt she was now old enough to help in some way. She read articles her father wrote for the Resistance and for underground newspapers, and she listened to his bold arguments with friends and relatives against Vichy France. She knew her older brother had joined the Free French forces in northern Africa and had walked across the Pyrenees (a mountain range) to unoccupied Spain with an underground group. Although she

helped in the war effort by working for the Red Cross, she desperately wanted
to do more.

> I was a volunteer and we had various jobs to do, mainly looking after chil-
> dren. Children were moved to safer places and we would pick them up at
> the train station and feed them and put them on a train to go south. If there
> had been a bombing, we would go and help the people in trouble or who
> had been shot or whose house had been bombed. There was not much
> bombing [in Paris], but alarms went out, and everyone was supposed to go
> to the cellar. But in lots of places in France, especially in Normandy, all the
> towns were devastated.

Shortly after her family moved to Paris, when she was 18 years old,
Andrée-Paule made a decision. She realized that with her youth as a disguise
and her Red Cross work as a convenient excuse to travel freely around Paris, she
would be useful to the Resistance.

Red Cross workers celebrate the liberation of Paris

I wanted to do something, so I made several contact friends and I helped in two networks. Of course, nobody knew about it. For one network I had an invented name, because everybody had an invented name, but for the other I didn't. I was always afraid, as I was still living with my family, that the Gestapo might come one day. I had to be very careful of this and, of course, I didn't tell anybody. I knew people around me who were deported and didn't come back.

Most Resistance fighters were not trained soldiers. Many, like Andrée-Paule and her father, were civilians who found themselves in the middle of a war. They often had to depend for their very lives on the ingenuity and quick thinking of others.

I was very lucky. I had a pass for the Red Cross because there was a curfew and you weren't supposed to go out after it. I had a special pass in case something was happening and I had to go and help. Somebody asked me, could I give them the pass, and they were later arrested with it and they swallowed the paper with my name on it.

Andrée-Paule delivered her messages by bicycle. Her contact person would give her a message, and she would type it, jump on her bicycle and deliver it. Sometimes she would deliver a message to a secret place where she needed a code to enter, and sometimes to another contact who would pass it on to someone else. Occasionally, she would provide an empty apartment for an important meeting.

Once I arranged a meeting to take place in my brother's flat [apartment]. These things were rather risky but people were risking all sorts of things. It was just a matter of luck, you could be arrested and deported . . . the entire family could have been in danger. . . . But I thought it was terribly important.

As part of her Red Cross work, Andrée-Paule was once sent to meet a train full of people who were being deported to a work camp. Under the guard of German soldiers, she was allowed to give each prisoner a drink of water. In desperation, the prisoners whispered phone numbers in her ear, and that night she called a few of their anxious relatives with their brief and final messages.

Gasoline was in short supply, and the cars that were driven by the privileged few used wood alcohol for fuel. People rode their bicycles almost everywhere. Food was also scarce in France. As in other war-torn countries, people used rationing coupons to buy food.

> I remember riding on my bicycle for a weekend in Normandy, trying to get some food. That was a great thing, to go on an expedition to get food . . . lots of young people went to see farmers to get a few eggs or some butter, and Jerusalem artichokes, which are a delicacy here, but we were just fed up with Jerusalem artichokes.

Some people—often through hoarding or stealing—obtained supplies of scarce goods and sold them for a profit. Andrée-Paule's mother once bought a large bag of gray macaroni through this "black market," and friends came by to take a pound or two each. It was a treat for everyone to have something other than the usual black bread.

> Everybody had a ration card . . . I was in an age group that wasn't allowed certain things that younger children were allowed . . . I remember fighting when I was working for the Red Cross, over some chocolates, with some relatives of mine, because chocolate was, my goodness, something extraordinary.

Andrée-Paule and her family listened constantly to the British Broadcasting Corporation (BBC) on their radio for news of the war. Interspersed with war news would be announcements like "the eggs are cooked," or "the carrots are burning," which were really coded messages for the Resistance fighters.

Following the invasion of Normandy in June 1944, and after fierce battles throughout northwestern France, the Allied forces allowed the Free French to lead the liberation of Paris. On August 25 of that year, the Resistance fighters were rewarded for their bravery.

> We were so excited when we heard that General Leclerc [a leader of the French army] had come into Paris. The south and that part of Paris was already liberated and all the church bells were ringing. We were still not liberated because where we lived was near the Arc de Triomphe, which was near the Majestic Hotel, and the Majestic Hotel was one of the headquarters of the German army, so we were still under German occupation for part of the day. I remember looking out of my window and seeing the Allied soldiers attacking the hotel and there was some fighting. Then the Germans

An American soldier and a French partisan crouch beside a car during a
street battle.

surrendered and the whole of Paris was liberated. It was terribly exciting, because one French soldier went up the Arc de Triomphe and hung out a huge flag, and that was something. . . . Then we all went to this big plaza and everybody was kissing. It was extraordinary. And then, at that time, all of a sudden, people started shooting . . . snipers!

Opposite, Parisians celebrating the liberation of Paris scatter for cover as German snipers open fire. *Right,* General de Gaulle's triumphant walk through Paris

Even in the middle of Liberation Day it was dangerous to be out on the Paris streets. The German soldiers were nervous and pointed their guns at the windows where flags from many countries were now draped. The French collaborators (people who had cooperated with the Germans), afraid of being captured by the Resistance fighters, panicked and, in the confusion, fired their guns into the crowds.

In Paris, American troops march down the Champs Elysees in a victory
parade, August 1944.

I remember lying down under the Allied tanks to avoid the shooting. . . . Even when General de Gaulle arrived a few days later, he walked from the Arc de Triomphe to Notre Dame [Cathedral] along with his staff, there were a few snipers. I took my bicycle and with a cousin followed de Gaulle and several times we had to take shelter because of snipers.

When Andrée-Paule looked back at her brave actions during the war, she said with conviction, "I wasn't a great Resistance hero, far from it, but I wanted to do something and I did what I could."

After the war, Andrée-Paule completed her education and became a volunteer for the American Red Cross. She was later a translator (she spoke German and English as well as French) at the Nuremberg Trials—the trials held in Germany to determine the role of German war criminals. She worked for the French delegation to the United Nations before joining the French Foreign Ministry's press and information department. She married David Mason, a foreign correspondent for the Associated Press, joining him in Vietnam during the Vietnam War. Later they were posted in Moscow for several years. Andrée-Paule died of cancer in 1991.

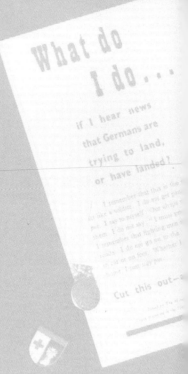

CLOTHING BOOK
1943-44 General

CUT ALONG THIS LINE

GLADYS GODLEY

Gladys Godley was born in Manchester, England, on April 19, 1934. She enjoyed the closeness of an older sister, grandparents, aunts, and uncles. When Gladys was five years old, England entered World War II. Germany had invaded Poland in September 1939, and England, in defense of its ally, declared war on Germany two days later. From the ages of 5 to 16, Gladys lived under the shadow of war and postwar disruptions.

Her first disruption was a major one—evacuation. When she was six, she was sent away for a year and a half to live with a family in a small town called Nelson, approximately 30 miles northwest of Manchester. Gladys was not alone. Two and a half million English children were taken by train to remote country villages. Many English people sent their children away from the cities, hoping they would avoid the worst of the German bombing. During the first week of the war, 4,000 special trains left from 72 stations in a mass effort to move the children quickly.

Between September 1940 and May 1941, the German Luftwaffe (air force) carried out a heavy bombing campaign, called the Blitz, on England. About 43,000 civilians—30,000 of them in London—were killed. The British Royal Air Force (RAF), though heavily outnumbered by the Germans, fought back courageously in what became known as the Battle of Britain. Eventually, heavy losses forced the Germans to concentrate on other fronts and abandon their efforts to destroy the RAF and invade England. The German forces surrendered unconditionally to the Allies on May 8, 1945. This event is referred to as Victory in Europe, or V-E Day.

We were taken to the station, which was dark. The train came in without lights. There must have been over 2,000 children standing on the platform waiting to go.

Gladys's mother had decided to send her away after a bomb had fallen on her grandpa's street.

Like several other houses on his street, Grandpa's house was split in half. Grandpa was sleeping and when he woke up, his bed was hanging over the edge and he was in it. My aunt Minnie, sleeping on the floor below and now covered with mounds of plaster, was terrified he would try to climb out of bed. "Don't get out of bed," she yelled. Grandpa, slightly deaf and disoriented, but otherwise unhurt, yelled back, "What happened to your hair? It is all white." And so it was, from the plaster dust. But they didn't care, they were so glad to be alive.

Gladys clutched her gas mask in its cardboard box and looked around the station platform. It was difficult to see anything, with only the moon for light, but the city was under a "blackout," meaning that all outdoor lights were banned. Heavy black shades covered all the house and store windows, streetlights were dark, cars could not use headlights, and even cigarettes were forbidden because the tiny glow of light they gave off might catch the eye of an enemy pilot.

Three-year-old twins take part in an evacuation test near West Kensington, London. The cardboard boxes contain gas masks.

The blackout became a part of life in England during World War II. The German Luftwaffe was bombing nightly, but the British resolved not to give the Germans an easy target—even if it meant curfew and darkness for months or even years.

Gladys was six years old. What had started out to be an exciting day was now a tiring and confusing one. She kissed her mother good-bye in the morning and set out for school as usual. But on this day, she was carrying a small pillowcase, in addition to her books and gas mask.

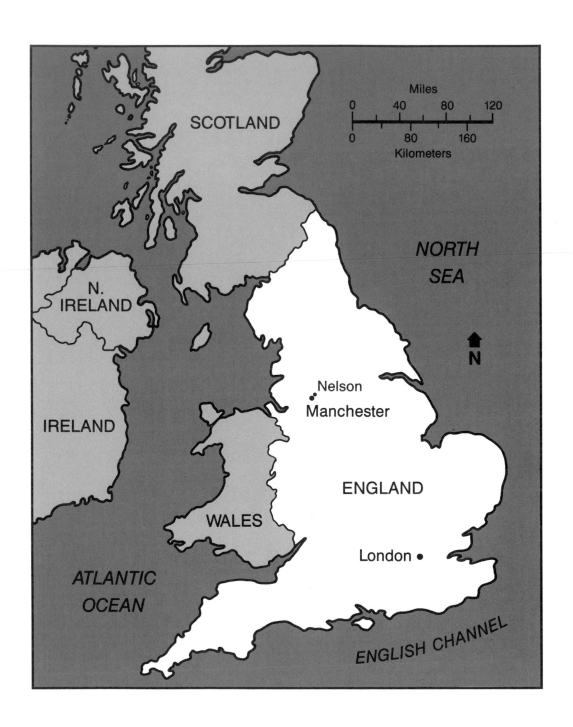

We all had a little cardboard box, and everyone was issued a gas mask. It was smelly rubber with metal at the front, but a gas attack was the one thing we feared the most. We found out afterward it was useless, but we treasured it. This was our lifeline, that little box with a string around it, everybody walked around with them.

Gladys's sister, Elfrida, was not going with her. Though only 16, Elfrida was old enough to get a job as a riveter in a factory. She helped make two combat airplanes—the Bristol Beaufighter and the Halifax bomber. In factories, offices, and on farms, thousands of teenagers and women took the jobs of the men who were fighting in the war.

Gladys looked at the label tied to her buttonhole. On it were her name and address, written in big letters. She wished she knew where she was going. Even Gladys's parents did not know where she would be. They would have to wait for a letter to arrive telling them where she was. In an attempt to keep the train routes secret from spies, neither children nor parents were told of the final destinations. On every street corner in England, there were posters with warnings, and the radio was full of messages cautioning citizens not to give war secrets away.

The train pulled into the station with its lights off. Six hundred children, ages 5 to 14, and their chaperones were loaded on. Each child had been given some orange juice and two sandwiches to eat on the train. Gladys found a corner seat and snuggled down. For two hours, the train sped through the countryside. As another security precaution, each town the train passed had its name on the station platform blackened out.

When Gladys finally reached the village of Nelson, her sandwiches had been eaten long ago, and her legs ached from sitting down too long. All she wanted was her warm home, her soft bed and, most of all, her mother. Instead, she was marched, with the small group of children left on the platform, to a bus that took them to a church hall. Children were going to church halls all over England to be "chosen" by their new families. Gladys sat down on the floor on the pillowcase that held all her possessions, and waited. All the children were on one side of the room, and the townspeople who had agreed to take them on the other side. They looked a bit suspicious, at first, of this somber lot of tired, disoriented children.

I looked a sight. I had black stockings on and my sister's clothes because they were a bit bigger than mine but warm, and a pink pixie hood because Snow White [the Disney cartoon] had been the great thing and every child had a pixie hood.

British troops arrive at a London railway station, as young evacuees depart.

Children sit amid the wreckage of their home in a London suburb.

But soon people were stepping forward and inviting the children into their homes.

"Would you like to come and play with my daughter? You could be a friend to Annabel."

Gladys looked up toward the voice. A lady and a girl about Gladys's age were standing over her. Gladys stood up, picked up her belongings, and followed the lady out the door. They walked past the town center, which was ringed with shops, to a small house on a quiet street. Annabel showed her the room they would share, and Gladys unpacked her bag.

Gladys's first letter home complained, "We had some soup and they put too much pepper in it." The government gave her foster mother a small allowance each week for her care. Much of their food was rationed, since the war disrupted both the farming and importing of food. The government rationed

Preparing for evacuation from London to the countryside

many kinds of food, ranging from meat and butter to canned fruit and breakfast cereal. Soap, razor blades, and gasoline were also rationed. Everyone was issued a book with coupons in it, and these coupons could be exchanged for one egg, four ounces of meat, and one ounce of cheese per person each week, and one block of chocolate per person each month. Potatoes, however, were plentiful and were served in endless variations.

With Annabel as her friend, Gladys started attending her new school. At first the local children did not like the evacuees. They thought that the way the city children dressed and talked was very different, but they gradually accepted their new classmates. The new village was quiet—there were no bombings, and everyone left their gas masks at home. Other than the peppery soup, Gladys found little to complain about.

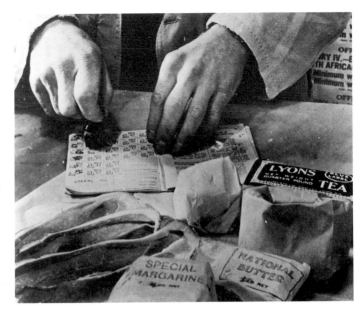

Right, A shopkeeper cancels coupons in a ration book. *Below,* A family enters their Anderson shelter.

Gladys was told by her foster family, "When you are fourteen we will get a job for you in the mill." Despite this prediction of a long war, Gladys stayed in Nelson only 18 months. She returned to Manchester at age seven and a half.

Other children were not so lucky. Many homesick evacuees returned home to risk the bombs rather than remain in their new homes. In some cases, hosts were unable to cope with the problems that arose when a stranger, or a family of strangers, landed in their midst. Some children were sent much farther away than the British countryside. Between 15,000 and 20,000 children were sent by ship to the United States, Canada, Australia, New Zealand, and South Africa. Most reached their destinations safely, but some were on ships that were attacked by German or Italian submarines. The worst casualties occurred aboard the ship *City of Benares*, which sailed for Canada from Liverpool, England, on September 13, 1940. Six hundred miles out to sea, the ship was torpedoed. Of the 300 people on board, 260 lost their lives. After this disaster, the British government banned any further evacuations by ship, leaving the 200,000 children still waiting to leave London with few alternatives.

About 300,000 children remained in London, and for them the war was an immediate and everyday part of their lives. Oblivious to the dangers, they would roam the bombed streets and rejoice in the upheavals, excitement, erratic school hours, and new hiding places created by the disorder and destruction. During the night, if they were lucky, they would sleep in their backyards in Anderson shelters—corrugated steel huts covered with dirt and capable of withstanding anything but a direct hit. When the Blitz started, the government had given away 2¼ million Anderson shelters, yet hundreds of households didn't have them. These families would descend each night into subway stations and claim a spot on the floor to lay their bedding. This was not an easy task, with hundreds of other people tossing, talking, reading, knitting, and even holding dance classes.

> Despite this, there was a marvelous spirit of friendliness. Everyone would turn their radio on and listen to Churchill saying the most incredible things. There was something about the timbre of his voice, the words he said. We were all willing to give "blood, tears, and sweat," because it seemed right. We were standing up for England.

Some families would line up for a bus or pile into their cars every night and drive out of London until they felt it was safe. There they would watch the bombing, sleep a little, and in the morning drive back home, ready to help clean up the damage or go to work.

After Gladys came home, the Blitz came to Manchester. Nearby caves provided refuge, and sometimes the entire town would disappear into them until an all-clear signal was heard.

> I was in an air-raid shelter, when suddenly the land went up and down, up and down, when the land mines [sic] were dropped. All of the windows in all of the shops and houses were out, and I went into our small backyard and picked up a large piece of shrapnel. I was quite thrilled. This was great. But we climbed out of the rubble to go to school . . . and at 3:00 every day the whole of Manchester and Stockport disappeared into the caves . . . sometimes it would be 18 hours before we would hear the all-clear signal.

This publicity photo was meant to encourage aluminum donations.

After Gladys's return to Manchester, food supplies became even more scarce.

I would queue up [line up] for food before I went to school and when I came back from school. The word was out that there were bananas in Mr. Jones's shop down the road. Queues stretched for blocks. We queued outside the butcher shop. The butcher was all-powerful as he stood there in his bloody apron. And in school we knitted seamed stockings [for the soldiers], out of horrible thick waxed wool. My fingers were torn and my socks never looked nice.

Gladys also learned about recycling. England had to depend on its own raw materials for most of its equipment, and supplies for the war always came before the needs of civilians. Since less lumber was being imported, paper was made out of rags, and even that was recycled. There were shortages of cloth, too:

Clothes went all around your friends and relatives. You shared everything. You learned to make do.

A clothing drive in London

Unloading aluminum at the British Ministry of Aircraft Production. Aluminum was melted down and used in the making of fighter planes.

The government—in need of cloth for soldiers' uniforms—saved hundreds of yards of material by prohibiting pockets, cuffs, and long shirttails on new clothing. Furniture production that used valuable timber was restricted, and toys made from plastics and rubber (resources needed for plane production) were banned except at Christmastime.

The war ended for England in 1945. There was cheering and dancing, and lights were blazing all over the country. But shortages continued for four or five more years. Gladys grew up during this time of continued rationing and restrictions. When an opportunity came along to be an airline hostess for the rapidly expanding airline industry, she enthusiastically accepted. For many years, she traveled around the world relishing the freedom and education her new job gave her. She is now married, has two sons, and is a magistrate (public official) for the City of London.

Not long ago, Gladys had an opportunity to speak to a group of people in Nelson, England, and she told them how she felt, as a six-year-old, coming to their village so many years before. When she told the part about the pink pixie hood, a white-haired, elderly woman spoke up. "Why, I remember you," she said. "You lived with my neighbor and her daughter. Welcome back to Nelson."

INOO FOREMAN

*I*noo Foreman was born on January 10, 1934, and adopted when she was one year old by the Reinhart family of Berlin, Germany. Her adopted father was a full-time soldier who had been wounded fighting for Germany in World War I, but recovered to fight again in World War II.

Germany had invaded Russia, a former ally, on June 22, 1941. The Germans were fighting on two fronts—on the eastern front (against Russia and the other countries to the east of Germany), and on the western front (against Britain, France, and other countries to the west of Germany). Inoo's father, a general, fought on the Russian front, where he was later captured and then imprisoned in Belgium. Inoo and her mother had to depend on each other during the war years.

Inoo watched the Hitler Youth, an arm of the Nazi party, recruit the children of Germany. Hitler banned most other organized clubs for young people and made membership in his youth organization mandatory, using it to spread his ideas of Aryan racial superiority. Hitler believed that Aryans—blue-eyed, blond

Caucasians—were the "master race," and all other peoples were inferior. Hitler arrested and killed any German who openly opposed his party. But by February 1945, Hitler was losing the war. The Russian forces were only a short distance from Berlin. Unlike England, Germany did not organize mass evacuations for people living in large cities, but instead encouraged them to leave of their own accord. Berlin fell to the Allies in April 1945, and on May 7, Germany surrendered.

After the war, both Germany and the city of Berlin were divided by the Soviet Union, Britain, France, and the United States into four zones of occupation. By the end of the 1940s, the Soviet Union had created a Communist political and economic system in East Germany and East Berlin, and it began to cut off all contact with the West. This division became known as the Iron Curtain, and resulting tension between the Soviet Union and the United States helped create the Cold War—the clash between the democratic governments of the West and the Communist governments of Eastern Europe. The nuclear arms race between the United States and the Soviet Union was one result of the Cold War.

In 1961, East Germans built a 20-foot-high wall separating the eastern and western sectors of Berlin. The wall cut the city in half and prevented free movement across what was once the busiest intersection in Europe. Many people tried to escape from East Germany to West Germany, and some died in doing so. White crosses marked the places on the wall where they fell. The most recent cross is dated February 6, 1989, just nine months before the historic date of November 9, 1989, when the Berlin Wall was torn down, signaling the end of the Cold War. For the first time in 28 years, the people of Berlin were allowed freedom of movement in a city that was once whole.

◆

We moved around [after the war] trying to get back to our flat in West Berlin . . . (my mother) stuffed herself with pillows to pretend she was pregnant, because then she would get better treatment. We did get safely into West Berlin and our flat was all right—but no furniture was there. Then the hard times really began.

Inoo watched her father's long face as he walked with a heavy step toward her. "Be good, *liebling*," he said, as he lifted her up for a gentle toss and a kiss. "I'll

Hitler's army invaded countries throughout Europe. Above, German police enter Austria in 1938.

be far off in Russia, but you and your mother will be fine here in Berlin, and I'll be home soon. The war won't last long." Inoo, having heard so much about Hitler's *Blitzkrieg*, believed her father would be back home again soon.

Inoo and her mother and father lived in a large flat near the Kurfürstendamm, Berlin's main shopping street. They were close to the Berlin Zoo, and most days after school Inoo and her father visited the zoo. She loved animals and knew she would miss these outings while her father was away.

As the weeks passed, Inoo noticed how troubled her mother looked. Inoo tried hard to cheer her up with stories she had heard from her friends about the Hitler Youth. Inoo was too young to join, but she tried to convince her mother to allow her to when she reached the age of ten.

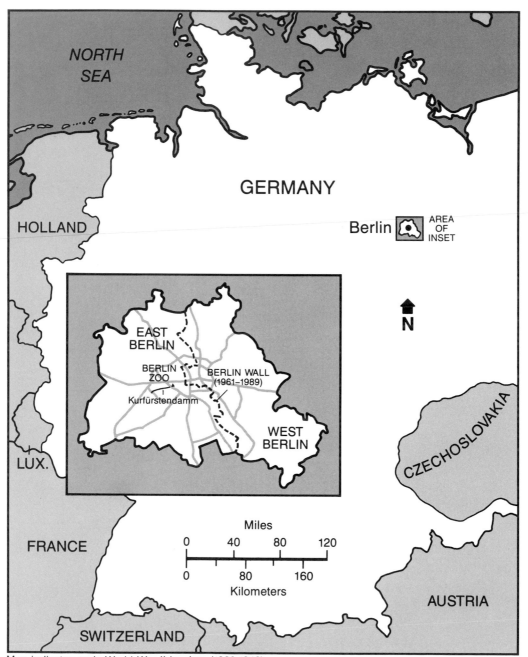

NORTH
SEA

GERMANY

HOLLAND

Berlin AREA OF INSET

N

LUX.

FRANCE

EAST BERLIN

BERLIN ZOO

BERLIN WALL (1961–1989)

Kurfürstendamm

WEST BERLIN

CZECHOSLOVAKIA

Miles
0   40   80   120

0   80   160
Kilometers

AUSTRIA

SWITZERLAND

Map indicates early World War II borders (1939-1942)

My mother did not like the Hitler Youth. I wanted to go because the girls had beautiful brown skirts and lovely ties and white blouses. They sang beautiful songs around the camp fire and did lovely things outside. I never realized about the politics, but my mother did know and she did not agree with that. Everybody had to go in and my mother was pestered by friends that I should go in, but my mother said no.

Inoo's mother was disturbed by Hitler's ideas. She was also well aware of the danger of arrest and probable execution to anyone in Germany who openly spoke out against the Führer (leader) or the Nazi party.

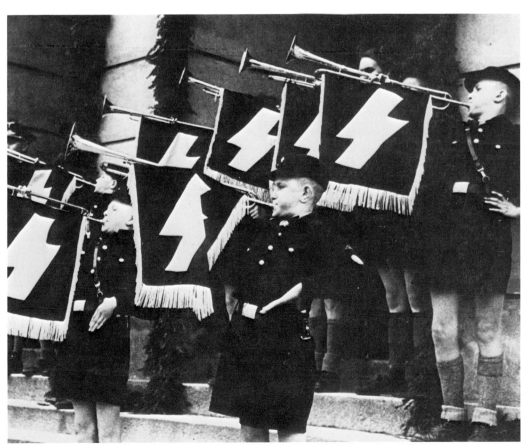

Hitler Youth

My mother listened during the war to the BBC, which was not allowed, so if you were caught, you would be carted off, and if any of your friends would know that you were listening to it, they could give you away. Children who were in the Hitler Youth have given parents away, because that's what they were made to believe was right.

Inoo could only listen to her friends' stories about the sporting activities and camping trips the members organized. By the time Inoo was ten, many of the sports facilities and clubhouses had been bombed, and many of the Hitler Youth leaders had become soldiers. A generation of children had been trained to obey the authority of the government over the family and to remain loyal to the "Fatherland" (Germany) above all else.

In spite of the war, life in Berlin continued as in peacetime. Plays, concerts, and operas were performed, and women still managed to have their hair done and to buy new hats and clothes. For those who were not Jewish, who contributed to the war effort, who did not speak against the Nazi party, and who could cope with a bewildering array of regulations, the early years in Berlin were almost peaceful.

Identification papers were important. People needed documents and certificates to prove who they were, where they lived, and even why they were walking on the street. Because Inoo was adopted, she needed to carry a certificate stating she was Aryan. Her mother was issued identity papers and ration cards that allowed her to purchase food for herself and Inoo each week. Work permits were issued to everybody, as were permits to buy clothing. Postal identification cards were needed to collect mail, and documents were required for leaving the city.

Many Jewish people in Berlin went into hiding in order to avoid being arrested. Since Jews were not registered and were not issued ration cards, sympathetic non-Jewish people, at great risk to themselves and their families, passed on supplies.

The first bombing raid on Berlin was on August 25, 1940. There were occasional raids until November 1943, when the Allies launched a major bombing campaign on the city. Inoo and her mother saw the destruction around them and slept in the cellar for safety.

We used to go into the cellar every night to be safe from the bombs. You could hear them whistling. Then, because the bombing was very heavy and large parts of the town were destroyed, we were advised to go to the bunker [a concrete building about 10 minutes away] every night. You heard the siren going, but of course you did not have time to go to the bunker. I was frightened in the cellar because we also had gas masks on. We could not breathe very well. We could hear the bombs crash and you wondered whether they had hit your house . . . it was nearly every night. I remember our street was burning on both sides—it was up in flames. I could see, up from the top, furniture falling, crashing down. . . . Our house had been hit, but luckily it wasn't burned out.

Berlin was almost flattened by the raids. Before the war, Berlin had 25,000 streetlights; 4,000 were left standing in 1945. There were burned-out buildings, large potholes in the streets, and piles of rubble everywhere.

A mother and daughter search for firewood in bombed-out Berlin.

In the rubble, nightshade used to grow, and nettles and weeds. We used to collect them and out of the nightshade we made jam. It was bitter because we couldn't get sugar. Only later we found out it could cause blindness. We were very lucky.

Streetcar and railway lines were destroyed, and riding a bicycle or walking became the only ways to get around the city. Water mains were broken, and people had to carry buckets of water from the street pumps back to their homes.

On November 24, 1943, a heavy bombing raid damaged the cages at the zoo. Many of the animals that Inoo had enjoyed visiting were injured and had to be shot.

Families seek shelter in Berlin.

An American army ambulance carries wounded soldiers through the German countryside.

Inoo and her mother knew that they could not stay in Berlin any longer. With hundreds of other families, they moved to outlying villages and farms.

> We took a lot of furniture away with us because we thought we might be safe there. It was a lovely time for me, very carefree because I loved the country, I loved nature, I loved to be with farm animals. It was a large farm we were on and there were horses and cows and sheep. I loved to bring hay in and jump in it. But the Russians came nearer and nearer and we had to run away.

Throughout Germany people were opening up their homes to those who had lost their homes or had fled the bombing. Inoo and her mother traveled from farm to farm, always having to leave—sometimes with their host family—when the Russians came too close.

We had a lot of horses and wagons and put some of our belongings on; my teddy was very important to me. We got to another farm and the people let us stay there. It was a Shetland pony farm and there were the most beautiful Shetland ponies. They used them for farming, they had little wagons and would plow the fields and also take people for rides.

But Inoo and her mother were forced to flee again, as the Germans retreated and the Russians moved forward.

The farm was in danger so we left our hosts and went farther . . . I remember once we slept in the woods and that was very exciting . . . it was summertime so we didn't freeze. It was beautiful to listen to the birds. My mother was uncomfortable, she knew all the dangers ahead.

A few days later Inoo was running along the road, ahead of her mother, when she suddenly felt herself being hurtled into the ditch.

You could see the planes coming, enemy planes . . . and those in the wagons had to get out. My mother threw me into the ditch and threw herself on top of me. I was peeping out from underneath her and it was a plane going very, very close. That was quite frightening, because I saw a man inside shooting at the wagons and at us.

In addition to dangers on the road and not knowing whether the family would ever be reunited in Berlin, Inoo's mother had with her a huge amount of money, which she hid in a purse under her clothes.

She had to take out of the bank quite a lot of money. She did that early enough, then she had to see that she didn't get robbed. She had a little bag which she wore around her neck and it went down to her tummy—she wore that under her clothes . . . later on we couldn't draw any money because the bank accounts were frozen.

Inoo and her mother continued traveling across the countryside, buying food from farmers and fleeing from the Russian soldiers. For a time they traveled with another mother and her daughter, eventually making it back to the Shetland pony farm, but all the ponies had been killed by the Russians. A kindly farmer gave them two cows and a wagon, so they continued traveling with the cows until they could no longer feed them.

We left the cows at a farm and we just had a hand wagon, that you pull along. And then the Russians caught up with us. We were sleeping in barns, with lots of other people . . . some Russians came in, holding a torch and shining it on the people who lay there. They stopped in front of my mother. I was terrified, but I prayed that no harm would come to my mother, and the soldier got up and walked away.

By February 1, 1945, the Russian forces were advancing across eastern Germany. In April of that year, Hitler committed suicide in his bunker in Berlin. When Inoo and her mother heard the news, they made their way back to Berlin. The Russian troops occupied the eastern part of the city and the rest of the Allies the west, and the border was difficult to cross.

With his mother pushing from behind, this German boy carries his family's remaining possessions through the streets of Verdingen, Germany.

We moved around trying to get back to our flat in West Berlin. That was very difficult . . . there was chaos in Germany. My mother managed to prove we had a pass and get into West Berlin. . . . We drove on a coal wagon on top of the coals and spent a night in a locomotive shed.

The war was over and Inoo and her mother were home, but they had no money left, no furniture or windowpanes in the flat, and very little food. They put boards over the windows and searched the streets for anything that could

A German woman flees a burning building in Seigburg, Germany, April 1945.

This sign—with its message in English, Russian, French, and German—shows the division of Berlin after World War II.

be used for firewood. Inoo's mother then found a way to support them. Some people still had Persian rugs, jewelry, and other luxury items that the Allied soldiers occupying West Berlin were happy to buy. Inoo's mother sold these items for a commission—a percentage of the sale. She and Inoo were still hungry, but at least they were able to buy food and household goods on the black market. One day Inoo's mother was able to take her to the theater.

> She had to queue up to get some tickets, and she was only able to get one ticket. She was behind a Russian officer and she said to the ticket agent, "Can my child go in and I will sit out?" The Russian turned around and he said, "You can have my ticket." The Russians were very kind toward young children.

The construction of the Berlin Wall in November 1961

November 1989—the fall of the Berlin Wall

At last they had news from Inoo's father. He was alive and had sailed out of Russia on the last hospital ship. He was now a prisoner in the hands of the British. Inoo and her mother moved to the country to be with him. There they found lodgings in an old castle by a lake, with several other families. Inoo made friends, went to school, and learned how to spin and weave cloth.

When Inoo was 19, she left for England, where she studied to become a nurse. While training, she came across patients with numbers tattooed on their arms—the identification process of the concentration camps—and she was reminded of the horrors of Hitler's Germany.

RUPERT WILKINSON

Rupert Wilkinson was born in England in 1936. In 1939 his family moved to the city of Manila in the Philippines, where his father managed the Theo H. Davies & Co. sugar-exporting business. He was also an agent for MI6, the British secret service agency. When war broke out in the Pacific area, Rupert's father became the liaison officer between General Douglas MacArthur, commander of the U.S. armed forces in the Far East, and the British government.

The Japanese government had been trying to expand its empire in Asia, much like Hitler was doing in Europe. Japan and Germany had become allies. On December 7, 1941, Japan declared war against the United States and the British Commonwealth, bombing Pearl Harbor in Hawaii. By December 10, Japanese forces had landed in the Philippines. On December 22, they began to advance toward Manila.

Rupert's father was forced to travel with MacArthur, leaving Rupert and his family alone in the Philippines. The American and Filipino forces retreated to the

Bataan Peninsula, while the Japanese began to bomb Manila. Manila fell to the Japanese on January 2, 1942. The American and Filipino forces held out at Bataan until the following April.

The Japanese took 12,495 prisoners in the Philippines, interning them in prisoner-of-war camps. Santo Tomas, where Rupert, his sister, and his mother were taken, was the largest civilian internment camp in the Philippines, housing up to 4,000 people. Although rules were strict and conditions unpleasant, surroundings were far better than they were in the Japanese prisoner-of-war camps for captured soldiers.

On January 9, 1945, American troops landed in the Lingayen Gulf, 107 miles from Manila. They reached the Santo Tomas camp 24 days later. The battles that followed for the liberation of the rest of the city almost destroyed Manila, but the Allies triumphed and the Japanese resistance ended on March 4, 1945.

We were in siege for a long time, but I remember thinking that we would not be killed. . . . When we got out, it was a small boy's paradise. There were soldiers, they were our guys.

Rupert Wilkinson was a skinny little boy who loved pranks and was full of mischief. His family was British and his mother had employed an English governess named Evie. "She never lost an opportunity to tell us she had been a governess to Danny, a Siamese prince," Rupert remembers.

Before Japan entered the Second World War, Rupert and his family lived a peaceful life in the Philippines. But toward the end of 1941, even five-year-old Rupert began to sense trouble in the air.

We were walking by a large plaza in Manila, filled with soldiers, marching, carrying weapons, and waving flags. They were shouting, "We are preparing for war to defend our country." A few weeks later I heard a siren. My father said there was bombing far away, in the hills. Then I saw large sections of pipe in the garden. My mother told me it would be buried in the ground and used as bomb shelters. . . . I realized war was coming. I remember seeing the river Passig burning. When Manila fell to the Japanese, the Americans had set fire to some enormous oil tanks. I didn't feel particularly afraid . . . I was too small to imagine ahead. I remember being fascinated

This photograph, which was captured from the Japanese Army, shows Japanese troops on Bataan, Philippines, in 1942.

because the oil spread onto the river and made the river look as though it was on fire.

On January 2, 1942, General MacArthur surrendered Manila to the Japanese to save it from destruction. When he left the Philippines, Rupert's father went with him. With her husband gone, Rupert's mother was left to look after the family in occupied Manila. Expatriates (non-Filipino residents, such as British and Americans) living in the Philippines had been ordered into internment camps for the duration of the war, and rumors ran rampant about the appalling conditions in Japanese prisoner-of-war camps. Unable to escape from Manila, the foreigners stuck together for support and protection. Even before they were sent to the internment camp, Rupert's mother often packed up her

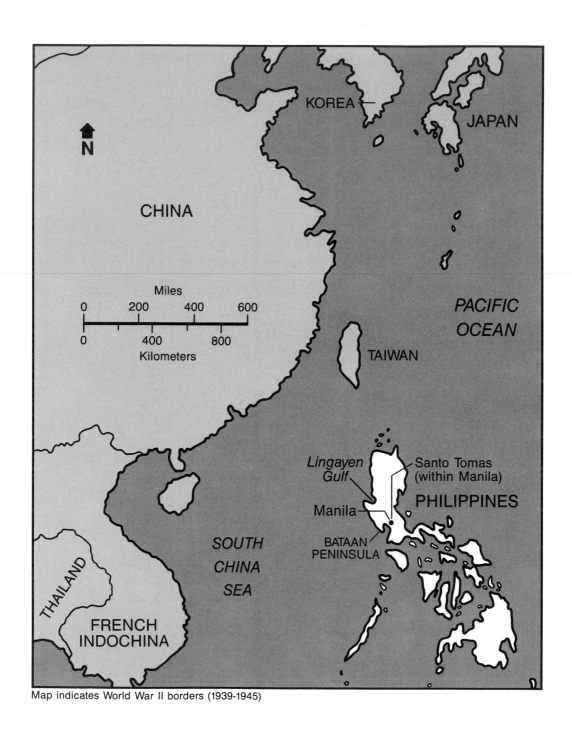

KOREA

JAPAN

CHINA

PACIFIC
OCEAN

N

Miles

| 0 | 200 | 400 | 600 |

| 0 | 400 | 800 |

Kilometers

TAIWAN

Lingayen
Gulf

Santo Tomas
(within Manila)

PHILIPPINES

Manila

BATAAN
PENINSULA

SOUTH
CHINA
SEA

THAILAND

FRENCH
INDOCHINA

Map indicates World War II borders (1939-1945)

family to spend the night with an Irish family, who were later arrested as war criminals and never heard from again.

Rupert was playing on his swing in the backyard when the Japanese soldiers came for them.

> We were told to stay outside and play while they interrogated my mother. We had been told the Japanese soldiers liked children, so Mary June [Rupert's sister] and I were not very afraid . . . we were just a little afraid. They looked tall to me in uniforms with peaked caps, and trousers tucked into boots . . . they were friendly, pushing us on swings. Meanwhile the officer was questioning my mother about what my father was doing, but they did not open the filing cabinet that held evidence about my father's activities.

Rupert, Mary June, and their mother each packed a suitcase and were driven by the soldiers to Villamore Hall, a large community center in the city. When they arrived, Japanese soldiers separated the men and boys from the women and girls. In the confusion, Rupert and his mother thought this might be the last they would see of each other. Rupert's mother remembers:

> We were all numbered off. The boys went with the men and that was the last I saw of Rupert. Things were going so fast. I got hold of one of my friends in the line and he said he would keep an eye on him. They all went downstairs and into trucks and we didn't know where they were going.

Rupert recalls:
> I thought I was going to be taken away from her forever. An older English boy, whom I had always rather disliked, a bossy boy, was suddenly very nice to me and . . . he put his arm around me and said, "Don't be frightened, we'll take care of you'" and that frightened me even more. I thought, "I have to be taken care of!" I remember being separated for 1 hour, but I am told it was 24 hours.

The separation was temporary, and when Rupert was reunited with his family, they were driven to Santo Tomas University in Manila. The campus had been turned into an internment camp.

Once there, Rupert explored. The camp was a large walled-in campus containing all the usual college buildings and facilities. At first everyone slept in classrooms, now lined wall-to-wall with beds. Later, boys eight and over were sent to sleep in the men's dormitory, where the internees soon organized a Boy's Club. Within a few months, wood and straw shanties were built, one for each family. The names given to each cluster, or "shanty town," such as Froggy Bottom (named after Foggy Bottom, an area in Washington, D.C.), often humorously described the homesick longings of the internees.

At first Rupert and Mary June spent their days together in their hut. But with very few books to read, no toys or amusements, they soon turned on each other.

> We used to fight. I thought she was bossy and she thought I was a mama's boy. I was faster but she was heavier and I used to tease her, annoy her, but as soon as Mum got to the hut I was as good as gold.

After a few weeks, interned teachers started a school. Mary June and Rupert joined the other children for daily classes, using whatever books, paper, and pens they could find. In theory, the school was a good idea, but the internees' biggest problem was hunger, and that soon made it impossible to concentrate.

This university gymnasium became a dormitory at Santo Tomas internment camp in Manila.

An American intern at Santo Tomas cooks the daily meal of corn-meal mush for her young daughters.

We became too hungry after a time. Breakfast was a kind of mush with coconut milk. Lunch was a very thin black soup with sometimes a hardtack [dry biscuit]. Supper was often a small dried fish, almost impossible to eat. This would be eked out with a small bit of corned beef from the comfort kits the Red Cross sent us.

Occasionally parcels from the Red Cross would arrive, containing canned corned beef, powdered milk, bars of dark chocolate, and packs of cigarettes. Rupert's mother would trade her cigarettes for more canned meat, and she optimistically saved one tin of canned meat for liberation day.

Washing hair in an outdoor tub at Santo Tomas

Americans liberated from a Japanese internment camp

Rupert's mother remembers:

Everyone had different theories of what was the best thing to eat. It was my theory that it was not good to have sugar, many people ate sugar to keep up their energy, but I didn't see what we needed energy for. Fat was the thing we wanted, and once in a while I could buy a tin of margarine with our "mickey mouse" money, as we called the old, useless Filipino money.

Keeping her children fed was Mrs. Wilkinson's biggest worry, but Rupert remembers boredom as his worst enemy. He read and reread all of his books and used every available bit of paper for drawing, mainly battle scenes and

A child's drawing of a hut in Santo Tomas

planes. He soon found a friend named Nick Balfour. Nick and Rupert would roam the camp, trying to stay out of the way of the older, tougher boys. If they met a Japanese officer, they had to bow their heads. They always had to remember the rules of the camp.

> The discipline was all or nothing. Basically the guards left us alone. But if you did something wrong, if you tried to escape, that was it, you would be killed . . . you would dig your own grave and then be shot. And if you received cans of food over the wall, that was also a capital offense. I only learned afterwards that, with great courage, a number of people we knew were secretly bringing food in by tunnel, under the wall. There was contact with people outside the wall, even though that was totally forbidden.

Despite the strict rules, a cautious rapport developed between the soldiers and the children. One day, the Japanese officers lost a wild pig they were keeping. They asked the Boy's Club to help them find it. Rupert and Nick were delighted to help, but a girl, Marion, and her friends actually found the pig.

> They [the girls] became very angry because we got all the credit and the Japanese gave each of us a molasses sweet and a colored T-shirt. We sat in front of Marion and her friends eating the candy and wearing our shirts.

Although radios were forbidden, several people had them, and news of the war filtered in. A second civilian internment camp, Los Baños, had been started in the hills outside Manila, and word reached Santo Tomas that the U.S. forces had staged a daring paratroop rescue of the internees.

Speculation about whether, and when, the Allied soldiers would rescue the Santo Tomas prisoners increased when two U.S. Air Force planes were spotted overhead.

Early in February 1945, gunfire reverberated over the walls. Unknown to the internees, 700 U.S. troops had been storming their way through 60 miles of Japanese-held territory to liberate Santo Tomas. After cutting through fields and fording rivers, they reached the gates of the campus. The tanks crashed through the gates, and cries of "They're here!" mixed with the grinding of the tanks coming up the main drive. Powerful flares outlined the muzzles of the guns on each tank.

One Japanese officer was killed and the remaining 65 Japanese guards fled to the first floor of the Education Building, a steel-reinforced concrete structure used as their base on campus. The U.S. troops, with all of their tanks, jeeps, water trucks, and ambulances, pulled up to the building and opened fire.

Mrs. Meredith, a friend of Rupert's mother, ran through the crowd, her pajamas flapping in the wind. "Do you realize our boys are in there?" she cried.

The Boy's Club slept on the second floor of the Education Building. Rupert and his friends were, by now, hiding under their beds and listening to the deafening roar of the gunfire.

> It sounded like a giant typewriter. I had a great tin trunk behind my bed, which I thought was wonderful protection. The Japanese gathered in the corridor behind us. One internee was killed by shrapnel or floor splinters. We were in siege for a long time [24 hours], but I remember thinking I

would not be killed. Then a truce was arranged and the Japanese were given safe conduct out of the camp. Under the truce, before they left, a great cauldron of hot corned beef stew came in, and it was delicious, we were so hungry.

When Rupert finally ran out of the Education Building, tanks, soldiers, and guns filled the familiar campus grounds. The internees were celebrating their release while the U.S. troops, exhausted, fell asleep in their tanks or under the nearest tree.

Rupert had been in Santo Tomas for two and a half years. It took several months for the Wilkinsons to find space on a ship, but by April 1945 they were sailing for California. Rupert's father was there to meet them. A few months later, the Wilkinsons left California and returned to war-torn England.

General MacArthur (center) returns to the Philippines on October 20, 1944, landing on the island of Leyte.

U.S. Coast Guard landing barges in the Lingayen Gulf carry the first wave of troops to the beaches of Luzon, Philippines, on January 9, 1945.

When we went home to Britain, I thought everything was gray and the cars looked old-fashioned [compared to the ones in the United States]. My father was cross with me and said, "Now look, these people have had a war."

Rupert's mother recalls:

I had a new fur coat, which we bought in New York, and when I reached England it stood out because the people there had almost nothing.

After three years' absence, Rupert started school, finishing his education years later in the United States. He now lives in London and teaches American studies at London University. He retains the sense of fun and tolerance that helped him through the years in the camp.

"I have no animosity toward the Japanese," remarks Rupert's mother, and Rupert says the same.

TOSHI MARKS

Lady Toshi Marks was born Toshiko Shimura on March 23, 1936, in Tokyo, Japan. She was the second of four children. When Toshi was very young, the family moved to Niigata, in eastern Japan. Her father was a successful businessman, and they lived comfortably until December 7, 1941—the day Japan bombed Pearl Harbor, an important U.S. air base in Hawaii. The Japanese had been trying to expand their empire for several years. In protest, the United States and Great Britain imposed restrictions on trade with Japan. Angry at these restrictions, which were making it difficult to obtain raw materials, Japan declared war.

At first, the battles between the Allies and Japan were carried out mainly on several islands in the Pacific. The Japanese controlled most of the Pacific until the Battle of Midway—a tiny island in the Pacific—when the United States blew up three Japanese aircraft carriers. A setback for the Japanese, this battle proved to be a major turning point for the United States.

The first extensive U.S. bombing raid on Japan was in June 1944. The American bombers concentrated on destroying aircraft factories and industrial areas. Later they stepped up their campaign and attacked Tokyo and other cities. They flew from bases in China and in the Mariana Islands.

On March 9, 1945, more than 300 B-29 bombers flew over Tokyo and dropped 2,000 tons of bombs. Strong winds created a firestorm that spread rapidly through the city, killing 84,000 people. By the end of May 1945, half of Tokyo had been destroyed, and several million people had been evacuated. The war ended when the United States dropped atomic bombs on the Japanese cities of Hiroshima and Nagasaki in August 1945. More than 200,000 people were killed and many more suffered terrible burns and lingering illnesses from the bomb's radioactive fallout. The Japanese surrendered on August 14, 1945.

With the end of the war came the occupation of Japan by U.S. forces, designed to stabilize the economy and reorganize the government along democratic lines. Japanese children used their old schoolbooks, but the pages that Americans found offensive were blacked out. Often there would be only a few words left on a page.

The occupation lasted six years. By 1952 Japan was an independent country with a democratic government and a figurehead (ceremonial) monarchy.

———————————◆———————————

We had no vision of the future, no hope for the future, just daily survival. Physically, mentally, we had to use every wisdom to survive, which is an amazing experience.

"Toshi, Toshi, come back here," said her mother. Toshi stopped skipping.

"Oh, no," she thought, "she is going to tell me I forgot my bubble."

"Toshi, you forgot your bubble," scolded her mother, Mrs. Shimura, that day in 1942 in Niigata. "You must carry it everywhere."

Toshi walked back to her house and found her bubble in the six-mat room, the large living area for her family. Her grandmother, who was sitting in the sunny eating area with Toshi's younger brother, gave her a smile as she walked out. She slung a white cotton padded hat, known as a bubble, over her back. All children in Japan had been given a bubble as protection against the American

Children on the island of Okinawa, Japan

bombs. The war was beginning to annoy Toshi. She walked to her school and thought about the bombing drills they practiced daily.

> A bell would go off and we would all rush off to wherever we had decided to 'escape' to. We wore bubble hats and also an ordinary cotton mask. It wouldn't help anything, it was a symbol. We had to go to a shrine once a month to pray for victory; at 6:00 in the morning we had to go and bow and we hated it.

In the early part of the war, Toshi did not pay much attention to it. Japan had been at war with China since 1937. War talk, to Toshi, was as natural as Sunday walks in the park, servants in her home, and vacations with her family. She was five years old on December 7, 1941, and only then did she notice the changes creeping into her routine.

> I first noticed the lamps being covered. And every night, the neighborhood man would walk around the house and see if there was any light peeking outside. Everything had to be blackened by paper or paint. I hated the

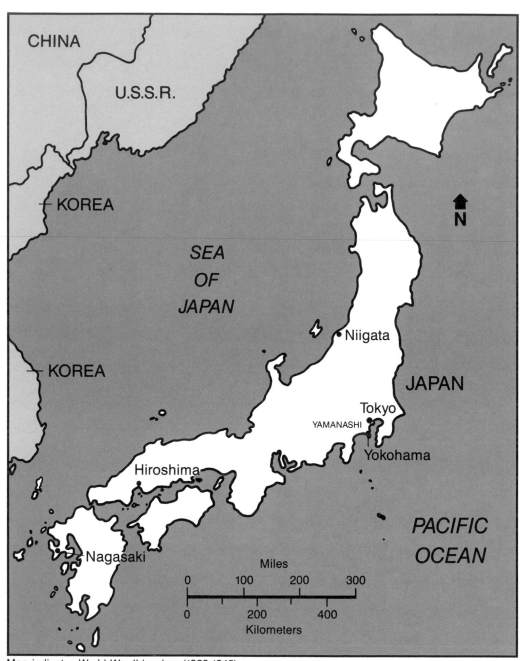

CHINA

U.S.S.R.

KOREA

SEA
OF
JAPAN

KOREA

N

Niigata

JAPAN

Tokyo

YAMANASHI

Yokohama

Hiroshima

PACIFIC
OCEAN

Nagasaki

Miles

0   100   200   300

0   200   400

Kilometers

Map indicates World War II borders (1939-1945)

lights being blackened because I always liked reading books, and at night everyone had to come to one room in the dark and you couldn't do anything. People shouted at you if a light was on. When I was sick, I would stay in bed and put a little light on and try to read, but someone always shouted. I didn't understand why they were doing that, I was too young.

Toshi noticed that every week, on every street, there was a neighborhood celebration in honor of a young man going off to war. The night before the soldier left, there would be a party. The next morning he would bow to each person, saying, "I am going now. Look after my family, I promise I will do well."

Toshi sometimes gave the soldier a cloth on which she had sewn hundreds of red dots. The soldier would wear it under his shirt, as a protection against bullets.

> Of course, it didn't work, but everybody had to do something for the war. It made us, even the children, aware. We also had to save up every resource to give to the government, cotton, paper, metal, everything had to go into the war. All our diamond rings went to the government to be melted. Everything had to be given away, the whole neighborhood was watching.

Japanese neighborhoods organized into groups, and the war effort became a joint responsibility. If one house did not obey the rules of the blackout, war donations, or neighborhood watches, all would be punished. One form of punishment was the withholding of food allotments. Even the children had to stand on the street corners asking, "Can you give something for my brother who is in the war?" so that they would not be labeled *hikokumin*, or anti-Japanese, and risk police harassment.

By the end of 1944, the Americans stepped up their bombing campaign, targeting the larger cities with their new B-29s. Because Japanese radio and newspapers were strictly censored, there was no international news. But in the final months of 1943, the Japanese people often spotted American planes flying overhead. Toshi was six when she left her comfortable home for a safer place in the country.

> When the bombing raids started in 1943, my parents decided to go back to my grandparents in their little village, Yamanashi, where there had been no

bombing. My father and older brother were called back to Tokyo to help in the war effort, and my grandmother, my mother who was pregnant, me, and my younger brother went to Yamanashi. We went by train, it took us three days and we didn't receive our belongings for three weeks. Even now, Yamanashi is one of the poorest parts of Japan, so we knew it would be hard to survive there.

Yamanashi is in a mountainous area east of Tokyo. Unable to grow rice—a staple of the Japanese diet—on this land, the people of Yamanashi survived on corn, soybeans, and a little wheat. Refugees from the bombed cities filled these remote areas, and the villagers had hardly enough to feed themselves. Fortunately, Toshi had relatives living in Yamanashi.

Struggling to survive in war-torn Japan

It was my grandparents' village, so we had some people willing to help us. But by 1943 food was strictly rationed. The first thing my mother did when she arrived was to plant. She had never done jobs like planting. Her cousin guided her, but it must have been hard.

Toshi's mother was quickly recruited for the neighborhood watch and was away from home for long days, rationing food and collecting war materials. Seven-year-old Toshi took on the responsibility of running the house and taking care of her younger brother and sister. At an age when she would normally have been attending school and playing with her friends, Toshi was baking bread and making soups and sugarless jams. Because there was so little wood for fires, baths were taken every two weeks, and the water was shared by 10 families. Toshi says her family was constantly cold, hungry, and filthy.

> I had to look after the children and cook the meals for them and for grandmother. This was extraordinary for most people, but not for us because by that time everybody was doing it. Had the war not broken out, we would have had maids, so we wouldn't have done that at all, but it wouldn't help to cry out or moan because we had to survive, that was all.

Toshi would strap her baby sister to her back, take her younger brother by the hand, and set out for the day. Food was scarce, and Toshi spent her days collecting firewood and looking for edible items in the mountains surrounding the village. Winter temperatures often fell to 15°F. Warm clothing had been confiscated for the soldiers, so Toshi and her brother had to forage in light clothing, without socks. Because of the weather, their poor diets, and the dirt, their skin cracked and bled, but hunger was their biggest problem.

> I was so hungry I went to the neighbors and asked if I could help them. They were farmers and always had little jobs to do. They would give me food, some I would eat and some I would take home to my family. I was always sent to the black market for food because children could escape more easily from that place. I might trade some vegetables for two cups of rice. Meat we probably ate once a year. Soon we started eating ordinary grass, leaves, anything because we were so hungry. We would boil everything and make a thin gruel soup. We were literally bones, the whole nation was starving.

Since there was no refrigeration for storing food, Toshi's family would boil everything, eat some, and dry the rest for later. Toshi's mother had never grown vegetables before, and her garden did not always do well. She was so proud of herself when she finally filled a small sack with sweet potatoes, but she stored them in the wrong place, and the potatoes turned rotten.

Occasionally sugar would be issued, and Toshi's family put it in a special jar. By mistake, someone once mixed salt with the sugar. They could only laugh about it. "We called it the disaster area, but it was serious because we needed both the sugar and the salt."

Hiroshima, Japan, in 1945. The arrow indicates ground zero—the exact point at which the atomic bomb exploded.

The ruins of Hiroshima

Once a month, Toshi's father would visit them, and he would tell them stories about the war.

By 1944, it was normal for him to see bombs everywhere. The person sitting next to him on the train was killed, or he walked halfway to Yamanashi without shoes because he had lost them in a bomb explosion, that kind of story. And by that time, most of the soldiers were killed. The government gave a letter to the family, and a box with nothing in it. We were not supposed to open it, but just bury it. Boxes started to arrive every day, somewhere in the village, so we all knew people were dying. And still we were told we were winning.

One day Toshi's father came to the house and Toshi's mother stepped onto their front porch to greet him. "Yokohama died," he said. He meant that the city of Yokohama had been bombed. Toshi's mother stood still for a moment. In a way, she was prepared for the death of her mother and younger brother. Because her brother was ill with tuberculosis, he could not be evacuated, so Toshi's grandmother stayed with him in Yokohama, their home outside of

Japanese children adjust to life after World War II.

Tokyo. Both were killed on March 9, 1945, when more than 300 B-29 bombers flew over Tokyo. "My father went to see," said Toshi. "He walked to Yokohama and found the house bombed and burned. Probably my grandmother and uncle jumped into the pump [well] in the backyard."

Until now Toshi had seen few planes, but by 1945, despite government broadcasts to the contrary, the war had come to Yamanashi.

> The Americans would come and 300 or more planes would fly over and bomb the town in the valley. The town was bombed for three days. It was quite big and there were ammunition factories there. Everything was black, completely dark all around. The town was burning for three days and

nights. . . . Between January and August of 1945, 8,000 planes were sent to bomb Japan. Less than 10 percent didn't come back, and even some of those were accidents. Only 50 planes were shot by Japanese, so you can see there wasn't anything in Japan at all to protect us.

In early August 1945, Toshi's father was sent home from Tokyo but was not told why. Like many people in Japan, he did not know that two major Japanese cities, Hiroshima and Nagasaki, had been destroyed by atomic bombs, which killed and burned hundreds of thousands of people. It wasn't until later that the Japanese people were told about the bombs.

> But you can't understand by writing that something crashes in one second and everything just disappears. No one believed such a bomb existed. People couldn't see it because there was no way to go there, no train, everything was destroyed, and the people who were there couldn't talk because they couldn't come out.

The atomic bomb not only killed instantly, it also left a lingering death—radiation sickness. Those that survived the sickness were left with yet another affliction: They "lost face," or felt ashamed, when Japan lost the war. The bomb victims were a reminder of the shame of all Japanese people, and they were shunned by society. The Japanese felt responsible for starting the war in the first place—by attacking Pearl Harbor—and therefore felt responsible for the dropping of the atomic bomb.

> The people who went through the bomb and suffered never blamed America. They felt ashamed. It is a very funny twist of the Japanese mentality, because they are ashamed because they are not healthy . . . because their children cannot marry properly, they feel they have a scar of the guilt. They are untouchable outcasts, you see.

On August 15, Emperor Hirohito, for the first time in the country's history, made a public broadcast to the people. The Japanese citizens knew the war was over and Japan was going to surrender.

> We were told we had to listen to the radio. We still didn't think that we were going to surrender. The Japanese never surrender, even in this situation, so we [thought that we] were having a special announcement,

encouraging us to continue. By that time, of course, we had no ammunition. All we had was a piece of wood, and we thought, we will fight with this piece of wood. At 12:00 the radio was on and we had never heard the emperor's voice before, he was god, but this funny voice came on and I didn't understand a word of it—he used very old, classic Japanese. My father said the war ended. Surrender, at that time, meant torture, because the Japanese are told not to surrender, if you do you have to commit suicide. The emperor said we must look to the future, which was telling us not to commit suicide, but to make a peaceful Japan.

Despite the emperor's pleas, hundreds of Japanese citizens committed suicide rather than accept defeat.

At the end of the war came the occupation of Japan by American forces. At first, Toshi was frightened of the American soldiers who came to the Yokohama port and found their way into her village. They had always been the

A Catholic home for war orphans in Kumamoto, Japan

enemy, and she thought she would have to hide in the mountains.

> This all changed when they moved into town. They had a smile and gave us chocolate and we realized the Americans didn't have horns, didn't have monstrous faces. . . . But as children, we had more of a shock than adults, because until the occupation we are told one thing, but after, we were told a totally different thing . . . now we must thank the British and Americans, that they are lovely. For a while, we stopped believing anything.

Toshi and her family stayed in Yamanashi for five years, finally moving back to Tokyo after her father's mother died. Life returned to normal very slowly. Even when food was again plentiful, she could not stop eating.

> Life was normal, but not normal. Children who felt starvation during the war had the symptom [the desire to eat] for a long time. Even when we had things, paper and pencils, we didn't want to use them, in case there would be another shortage. But the hard times came equally to everybody. Physically, mentally, we had to use every wisdom to survive. If it happens to you, it is an amazing experience. If you, as a child, have to take responsibility for your own existence, you become more aware of what you are doing. Children are amazingly strong . . . if they have to do the practical everyday things, they can.

When Toshi returned to Tokyo, it was hard for her to follow the traditional Japanese customs. She had survived a devastating war that had brought defeat, starvation, and political upheaval to her country. It had left four members of her family dead and her baby sister in poor health. Toshi was 15 before she felt free from the constraints and effects of the war. As a child before the war, she had spent every penny she could on books and would hide away for hours reading. The war and, for a while, the occupation had deprived her of reading, studying, and learning, but instilled in her a realization that she was capable of overcoming almost any adversity. With only belated help from her family, Toshi refused to take the path of the traditional arranged marriage, instead continuing with her education and obtaining a doctorate in economics. Today she lives and works in London, and still maintains, with great feeling, that children are amazingly strong.

When and Where

	1938	1939	1940
Hans b. 1928	*Kristallnacht*	Hans, Oscar, and Elsbeth flee to Holland.	Hans and Oscar escape to Britain.
Andrée-Paule b. 1923			Living in Hungary. Armistice in France.
Gladys b. 1934			Evacuated to Nelson.
Inoo b. 1934		Inoo's father leaves to fight in Russia.	Bombing of Berlin begins.
Rupert b. 1936		Rupert and his family arrive in the Philippines.	
Toshi b. 1936			

1941	1942	1943	1944	1945
				Elsbeth is released from Auschwitz.
Living in Sweden.	Moves to Paris with her family.	Joins the French Resistance.	France is liberated from German occupation.	
Returns to Manchester where bombing is heavy.				VE Day.
		Inoo and her mother flee Berlin for the countryside.		Inoo and her mother return to Berlin.
Japanese forces land in the Philippines.	Rupert, his mother and sister are sent to Santo Tomas camp.			U.S. troops liberate camp internees.
Japan bombs Pearl Harbor and declares war on U.S.		Toshi and her family flee to Yamanashi.	U.S. bombing of Japan.	U.S. drops atomic bombs on Hiroshima and Nagasaki.

Index

Acknowledgments

I have interviewed seven people for this book, six of whom spent a good portion of their childhood, or late childhood, directly involved in the most devastating war this world has known. These children, due to circumstances beyond their control, found themselves in conditions of upheaval, deprivation, and great uncertainty. All of them, at one time or another, mentioned how lucky they had been, and indeed they were. But they also had a determination to use their luck, and a clear realization that life involves choices.

By luck, by spirit and conviction, these people are survivors, and they represent the part of all of us, the survivor part, that would emerge were we to find ourselves in similar situations.

I would like to thank: Focus Information Service; Allison Day; Richard Tames; The Japanese Embassy; Caroline de Navacelle; Fr. Jacques Coupet; Gladys Godley; and Tibor Fülopp.

Trish Marx

Photo Credits

Photographs on the following pages courtesy of: Bettman Archives, p. 17; Bettman/Hulton, p. 2, 37, 42, 55; Bildarchiv Preussischer Kulturbesitz, p. 13, 14; Cleveland Public Library, p. 16, bottom, 31, 43, 46, 70, 72; German Information Center, p. 63; Imperial War Museum, p. 45, 47, 73; Library of Congress, p. 43; National Archives, front and back covers, p. 12, left, (W+C #981), p. 12, right, (W+C #985) p. 16, top, (W+C #1109), p. 18 (W+C #1104), p. 23 (W+C #998), p. 26 (#111-SC-193422), p. 29 (W+C #1055), p. 30 (#1057), p. 32 (W+C #1059), p. 40 (W+C #1013), p. 41 (W+C #1009), p. 51 (W+C #989), p. 53 (W+C #911), p. 56 (#111-SC-#204-322), p. 57 (W+C #1326), p. 59 (W+C #1258), p. 60 (W+C #1092), p. 61 (#11-SC-609868), p. 62 (#111-SC-587624), p. 67 (W+C #1140), p. 76, 77 (W+C #1206), p. 84 (#80-G-495629), 86, 87, p. 90 (W+C #1271); United States Holocaust Museum, p. 15; UPI/Bettmann Archives, p. 9, 71, 81, 88, 95. Maps and chart by Laura Westlund. Illustrations by Darren·Erickson.

Special thanks to Richard Trombley for photos on pages 6, 20, 34, 48, 64, and 78. Thanks also to the Holocaust Center at the Minneapolis Talmud Torah; After the Battle; Darren Erickson; and Kathy Raskob.